CORPORATE RELIGIOUS FREEDOM

CORPORATE RELIGIOUS FREEDOM
AND THE
RIGHTS OF OTHERS

Calibrating Human Rights in Times of Pluralist Dilemmas

Jeroen Temperman

Published, sold and distributed by Eleven International Publishing
P.O. Box 85576
2508 CG The Hague
The Netherlands
Tel.: +31 70 33 070 33
Fax: +31 70 33 070 30
e-mail: sales@elevenpub.nl
www.elevenpub.com

Sold and distributed in USA and Canada
Independent Publishers Group
814 N. Franklin Street
Chicago, IL 60610, USA
Order Placement: +1 800 888 4741
Fax: +1 312 337 5985
orders@ipgbook.com
www.ipgbook.com

Eleven International Publishing is an imprint of Boom uitgevers Den Haag.

ISBN 978-94-6236-913-9

For Irene, Samuel, Jonathan

ACKNOWLEDGEMENTS

This text draws on the public lecture I gave on the 1st of March 2019 at Erasmus University Rotterdam, thus inaugurating my chair in International Law and Religion in Interdisciplinary Context. My thanks goes to the Rector Magnificus of Erasmus University Rotterdam and the university's executive board, as well as to the Dean and Vice Dean of Erasmus School of Law, for the trust placed in me by offering me a professorship in international law and religion. Thank you to Wibren van der Burg and Peter Mascini, who have been generous with their time and provided excellent feedback on earlier drafts of this text. Thanks to Marco Ventura, for hosting me during my 2018 sabbatical at the Center for Religious Studies (ISR) at Bruno Kessler Foundation (FBK) in Trento and at the law school of the University of Siena, where the first inklings of my thinking about corporate religious freedom saw the light of day – thinking that gradually matured thanks to conversations with him and his colleagues at both institutes. Special thanks and gratitude to Ellen Hey, who tirelessly coached me through the academic ranks.

TABLE OF CONTENTS

1. INTRODUCTION

Imagine: A private company is incorporated under the laws of a liberal democracy. It is a closely-held company with relatively few shareholders. The owners – since times immemorial essentially a family-dynasty – have in common a shared religious affiliation which religious ethos they seek to imprint upon the way they go about their commercial business. Imagine furthermore that for those very religious reasons the company refuses to recruit persons of other faiths for senior executive functions. The company considers extending this recruitment policy to junior positions and all non-core jobs, including janitors, cleaning personal and caterers, with a view to maintaining a homogeneous religious ethos throughout all branches of the company.

Imagine: A member of the LGBT (lesbian, gay, bisexual and transgender) community enrols at a for-profit educational institution that provides legal training but is barred as per the institution's compulsory code of conduct that stipulates among other things that enrolled students may only engage in sexual acts when married; the country concerned does not recognize same-sex marriage.

Imagine (finally): A private company, incorporated under the laws of an EU country, specializes in organizing events. Competitively speaking, the company has recently been losing ground. Some clients have repeatedly complained about the company's catering personnel wearing religious dress or symbols and have warned they will seek an alternative provider or have already done so. At a board meeting of the company a policy of religious neutrality is adopted: henceforward the company is expressly secular, pursuing a policy of neutrality, and one consequence of this is that employees are forbidden from displaying their religious affiliation. The company feels that this policy change serves not only the vital interest of neutrality but also to protect its corporate image.

If you think I have a wild imagination concocting such scenarios, I should point out each of these examples is true to life, representing a mere sample of vastly proliferating conscientious claims in the corporate world. With a touch of drama one might refer to our age as the new 'conscience wars',[1] alluding to the current development that no longer only fringe religious minorities but also congregations of the formally hegemonic world religions are experiencing a sense of persecution – whether justly or with an ever higher touch of drama[2] – inflicted through secular-liberal agendas adopted at a global and local level. These wars are battled out, increasingly, before secular courts and the legislator. Such conscience claims are characterized by demands to be exempted from equal treatment or other generally applicable laws and are typically framed in terms that defy compromise. Secular individuals or entities, in turn, may marvel at the 'privileges' religious factions acquire using human rights law

---

1   E.g. Douglas NeJaime and Reva B. Siegel, 'Conscience Wars: Complicity-Based Conscience Claims in Religion and Politics', 124 *Yale Law Journal* 2516 (2015); Susanna Mancini and Michel Rosenfeld (eds.), *The Conscience Wars: Rethinking the Balance between Religion, Identity and Equality* (Cambridge: CUP, 2018).

2   E.g. Douglas W. Kmiec, 'Same-Sex Marriage and the Coming Anti-Discrimination Campaigns Against Religion', in Douglas Laycock et al. (eds.), *Same-Sex Marriage and Religious Liberty: Emerging Conflicts* (Rowman & Littlefield, 2008).

and may feel inclined to exert their secularity using the same legal framework.

The problem statement I wish to table can be broken down into the following queries: From the perspective of international law, can a private commercial company be deemed to be 'religious'? That is, is it possible for corporate entities to have, adopt and manifest a religion or belief? Does this include non-theistic and non-metaphysical beliefs such as atheism or agnosticism? And if so, do any such corporate beliefs merit the protection of human rights law? That is, if we accept companies can be based on a religious ethos, or conversely on an expressly non-religious ethos, may such business enterprises count on standards of fundamental rights to protect them in those instances in which their corporate religious ethos is threatened by actions of the state or individuals? If such a right at all exists, what is the scope of corporate religious freedom? And if corporate religious freedom collides with the fundamental rights of others, how do we equitably judge whose freedom is to prevail? And if freedoms are to be limited in the interest of the rights and freedoms of others, what arguments stand the legal tests of necessity and proportionality?

2. COLLECTIVE RELIGIOUS FREEDOM

Let us commence with a brief taxonomy of religious freedom. Is it an individual right? Is it a group right?

2.1 STANDARDS

From the outset of the modern human rights era, the internationally codified right to freedom of religion or belief, although a right enjoyed by individuals, has a collective dimension. The 1948 Universal Declaration of Human Rights (UDHR) provides that '[e]veryone has the right to freedom of thought, conscience and religion; this right includes freedom … *either alone or in community with others and in public or private*, to manifest his religion or belief in teaching, practice, worship and observance.'[3] Two decades later the UN Covenant on Civil and Political Rights (ICCPR), ratified by some 170 States, underscored this collective dimension in a nearly identical fashion.[4]

---

3   UDHR, Art. 18 (emphasis added).
4   ICCPR, Art. 18. Other human rights treaties, like the regional European Convention on Human Rights (Art. 9), follow a similar nomenclature of individual religious freedom with a profound collective dimension. The non-binding 1981 UN Declaration on the Elimination of All Forms of Intolerance and of Discrimination Based on Religion or Belief fleshes out the community dimension through recognition of a set of rights beneficial to organized religion (e.g. the freedom to collectively worship and assemble and to establish and maintain places for these purposes, the freedom to establish and maintain appropriate charitable or humanitarian institutions, or the freedom to solicit and receive voluntary financial and other contributions; Art. 6, sub (a) – (i)).

Remarkably, while virtually each and every aspect of the religion clause was considered controversial by the drafters of the International Bill of Rights and led to extensive and intense debates, the communal aspect of this right was rather straightforwardly codified. The formula 'either alone or in community with others' can be traced to British and French proposals.[5] The *travaux préparatoires* reveal that only the Soviet Union somewhat grudgingly acquiesced in the mounting consensus behind the community aspect of religious freedom. (Incidentally, somewhat of an irony is that today the Russian Federation is champion of the collective religious conscience of the Russian Orthodox Church, while France may perhaps not be hailed as the standard-bearer for public and collective manifestations of religion.)

Accordingly, for the vast majority of drafting delegations collective manifestations of religion – the possibility to freely engage with fellow believers and to practise religion in a communal fashion – was deemed part and parcel of the individual right to religious freedom. One representative, Dr Malik of Lebanon, went as far as positing that 'the words "either alone or in community with other persons of like mind" would bring out the idea that the Church was a *corporate body* and had an *inherent right* to propagate its doctrine'.[6] Such outspoken views, however, rather overstepped the mark as far as other drafters were concerned and any proposal to bestow explicit rights upon collective religious entities proved unsuccessful. Vesting too much

---

5   E/CN.4/AC.1/3/Add.3 (1947), p. 5: UK proposal for an 'International Bill of Rights', proposing the words 'either alone or in community with other persons'. The drafting debates concerning the ICCPR specifically settled on 'in community with others' via a French proposal and several amendments. E/2256 (1952), para. 233; and E/CN.4/L.155 (1952).
6   E/CN.VAC.3/SR.5 (1947), p. 9.

legal power and recognition in religious institutions per se might constitute a threat to public order, especially since organized religion, so it was felt, is bound to exploit such legal powers with a view towards proselytism (i.e. attempting to convert someone into a religion or belief).[7]

2.2 CASE LAW

Some of the remaining indeterminacy on the part of international human rights treaties in relation to collective religious freedom has been belied by international human rights monitoring bodies, which have not only acknowledged but also gradually extended the scope of this freedom. For instance, the UN Human Rights Committee – the body that monitors state parties' compliance with the ICCPR – has gone out of its way to recognize important aspects of collective freedom of religion. In the case of *Sister Immaculate Joseph and 80 Teaching Sisters of the Holy Cross of the Third Order of Saint Francis in Menzingen of Sri Lanka v. Sri Lanka*, the Human Rights Committee acknowledged the right of religious groups to acquire incorporated status.[8,9] This right is crucial to, for instance, the construction of new places of worship and other acts in relation to disseminating knowledge of the faith. (Incidentally, the Human Rights Committee is strictly incompetent to review claims brought by collective legal entities, including churches; as a consequence, relevant complaints before this body make for fantastic – if somewhat convoluted – case titles.)

---

7   A/2929 (1955), para. 116 (annotations on the draft Covenant by the then Secretary-General).
8   Communication No. 1249/2004, 21 October 2005, paras. 7.2-7.5.
9   Read in conjunction with the non-discrimination clause. ICCPR, Art. 26.

A notion only tangentially alluded to in the recorded drafting history,[10] it is the norm of *religious autonomy* that forms a chief rationale for recognizing the existence of collective religious freedoms and the state's duty not to unduly interfere with the internal realm of organized religion. The European Court of Human Rights in particular has held time and again that the 'autonomous existence of religious communities is indispensable for pluralism in a democratic society' because if 'the organizational life of the community [were] not protected by' the right to freedom of religion or belief, 'all other aspects of the individual's freedom of religion would become vulnerable'.[11] In its exegesis of the words 'alone or in community with others', the European Court of Human Rights reads the religion clause in direct conjunction with the freedom of association: 'Seen in that perspective, the right of believers to freedom of religion ... encompasses the expectation that believers will be allowed to associate freely, without arbitrary State intervention'.[12] Unlike the UN Human Rights Committee, the European Court granted churches and other collective religious entities standing to bring complaints to Strasbourg decades ago, a possibility that has created a vast body of case law – some 300 cases to date – concerning alleged undue state inference with collective religious manifestations.

---

10 E.g. E/CN.4/AC.1/SR.10 (1947), p. 10: 'the notion of the autonomy of religious sects and orders' (Malik).

11 *Hasan and Chaush v. Bulgaria*, No. 30985/96, 26 October 2000 (GC), para. 62. See also e.g. *Metropolitan Church of Bessarabia and Others v. Moldova*, No. 45701/99, 26 October 2000 (GC), para. 118; and *Sindicatul 'Păstorul cel Bun' v. Romania*, No. 2330/09, 9 July 2013 (GC).

12 *Church of Scientology Moscow v. Russia*, No. 18147/02, 5 April 2007.

Legal scholarship, too, shows strong support for the axiom that securing the collective dimension of religious freedom is crucial to the realization of individual religious freedom.[13] Legal theory arguments in support of a comprehensive notion of collective religious freedom range from pointing to practical obstacles religious groups would face in the absence of such a freedom (e.g. acquiring assets and performing other vital legal acts would become burdensome if not impossible),[14] to pointing out that the confining of religious freedom protection to the privatized realm of the individual would inevitably cause major religious freedom restrictions since the community aspect of religion for many practitioners is an integral part of religious practice,[15] to underscoring the value of the internal religious autonomy of religious communities per se.[16]

---

13   See also Carolyn Evans, *Freedom of Religion under the European Convention on Human Rights* (Oxford: OUP, 2011), pp. 103-105.

14   W.A. Schabas, *The European Convention on Human Rights: A Commentary* (Oxford: OUP, 2015), p. 429; Patrick Thornberry, *International Law and the Rights of Minorities* (Oxford: Clarendon Press, 1991), p. 152.

15   Y. Dinstein, 'Freedom of Religion and Religious Minorities', in Dinstein (ed.), *The Protection of Minorities and Human Rights* (Dordrecht: Martinus Nijhoff Publ., 1992), p. 152; Cornelis D. de Jong, *The Freedom of Thought, Conscience and Religion or Belief in the United Nations (1946-1992)* (Antwerp/Oxford: Intersentia/Hart, 2000), pp. 253-254.

16   Merilin Kiviorg, *Freedom of Religion or Belief: The Quest for Religious Autonomy* (PhD dissertation, University of Oxford, 2011).

3. CORPORATE RELIGIOUS FREEDOM

There is no denying that international human rights standards carve out a significant collective dimension for the right to freedom of religion or belief. The fact that religious freedom can be exercised both alone and 'in community with others' has been taken to mean that collective religious entities, like churches and other religious organizations, are separately recognized as rights holders along with their individual members. When harmed, these religious organizations may have standing in front of some international monitoring bodies – within Europe notably the European Court of Human Rights – to vindicate any undue interference with their religious autonomy. Crucially, now, for our discussion is the extent of such 'rights-holdership'. That under international law collective religious freedom would affect the protected status of churches and religious organizations is only to be expected given that the collective exercise of religious freedom in church-like settings is an indispensable part of individual religious manifestations in many religions. But what happens to that protected status if the collective religious manifestation at stake is taken out of the physical house-of-worship context? Can other organizational structures, above and beyond churches and religious organizations per se, be deemed to 'be religious'? And if so, do such collective entities qualify for religious freedom protection? Specifically, do commercial companies based upon a religious ethos enjoy religious freedom?

While the church and its direct offshoots, i.e. not-for-profit
branches with a profound religious mission in the charitable
or humanitarian field,[17] are recognized rights holders, positive
international law and the *travaux* are silent on the question of
commercial companies as holders of religious freedom. Any
indication as to the existence of relevant ownership of rights by
companies must be sought in such secondary sources as international case law and legal doctrine. As the latter is rather scant,
let us focus on case law.

As previously noted, due to the standing of collective legal entities, the European Court of Human Rights (including the former
European Commission of Human Rights) has been in a position
to rule on relevant cases more often than some of the other monitoring bodies. I distinguish five phases in the Court's case law:
1. In the early case law – 1960s and most of the 1970s – 'Stras-
    bourg' was adamantly averse to any notion of corporate
    religious freedom; indeed, it was opposed even to churches
    per se being regarded as beneficiaries of religious freedom.
    Accordingly, in *C. of S. v. United Kingdom* (1968), a case
    brought by 'a corporation incorporated under the laws of the
    State of California' (the anonymized decision does a poor
    job of hiding the fact that the Church of Scientology was the
    complainant corporation)[18] it was ruled 'that a corporation,
    being a legal and not a natural person, is incapable of hav-
    ing or exercising [religious freedom]'.[19] The decision is all the

---

17 UN 1981 Declaration, Art. 6(b) ('charitable or humanitarian institutions').
18 *C. of S. v. United Kingdom*, No. 3798/68, decision of 17 December 1986, The Facts.
19 *Ibid.*, The Law.

more striking since corporations could at the time enjoy such Convention provisions as fair trial rights. The impossibility of churches, let alone companies, possessing religious rights was the dominant line of case law until the late 1970s and was reiterated in freedom *from* religion cases too. One such case was brought by a limited liability company (LLC) offering printing services. The company complained that the Swiss Canton where it was incorporated forced all private companies, regardless of their founders' religious affiliations, to pay ecclesiastical taxes – paying of such 'tithes' is common under state church regimes – in favour of the *Landeskirchen* (cantonal state churches). 'Strasbourg', however, stuck to its guns and reiterated that an LLC, 'given the fact that it concerns a profit-making corporate body, can neither enjoy nor rely on [religious freedom]'.[20]

2. A second phase commenced in the late 1970s and early 1980s. In a case against Sweden brought by the Church of Scientology, the Commission reversed the case law of phase one, stating that it 'is now of the opinion that the [previously-made] distinction between the Church and its members under [the right to freedom of religion or belief] is essentially artificial. When a church body lodges an application under the Convention, it does so in reality on behalf of its members. It should therefore be accepted that a church body is capable of possessing and exercising [religious freedom] in its own capacity as a representative of its members'.[21] Promising though that sounds for collective religious freedom, the Commission makes an important caveat: religious freedom under the European Convention 'does not confer protection'

---

20 *Company X. v. Switzerland*, No. 7865/77, decision of 27 February 1979.
21 *X. and Church of Scientology v. Sweden*, No. 7805/77, decision of 5 May 1979.

on manifestations of purported religious belief that are of a 'purely commercial nature'.[22] And that was precisely what the applicant was engaged in: commercial dealings. Specifically, the Church of Scientology had placed an advertisement marketing its so-called 'E-Meter', a religious artefact 'used to measure the state of electrical characteristics of the "static field" surrounding the body and believed to reflect or indicate whether or not the confessing person has been relieved of the spiritual impediment of his sins'.[23] Offering the device for sale to the general public – with a discount for Scientology members – the advertisement insisted that '[t]here exists no way to clear [yourself] without an E-meter'. Once the Swedish Ombudsman started receiving complaints – for the E-meter does not work – the Church was ordered by a court to amend certain passages of the commercial. To sum up, while the Commission made a major U-turn in accepting that corporate entities have standing to plead collective religious freedom on behalf of their members, commercial activities were at this stage barred from the scope of the protection.

3. The third phase further augments and extends the standing of faith-based organizations to invoke the European Convention's religion clause. In addition to church bodies per se, according to the European Commission of Human Rights in the early 1980s, any 'association with religious and philosophical objects' 'is capable of possessing and exercising [religious freedom]'.[24] Accordingly, atheist, agnostic, humanist, etc., incorporated entities, too, were declared fit to exercise the right to freedom of religion or belief.

---

22 *X. and Church of Scientology v. Sweden*, The Law.
23 *X. and Church of Scientology v. Sweden*, Summary of the facts.
24 *Swami Omkarananda and the Divine Light Zentrum v. Switzerland*, No. 8118/77, decision of 19 March 1981.

4. Whereas for some years 'Strasbourg' dodged the crucial question as to whether associations' objects must be purely religious or philosophical or that commercial activities may be part of the mission statement in order to be eligible for religious freedom protection, late 1980s case law brought a major blow to the notion of corporate religious freedom. Specifically, collective legal entities were denied standing when bringing *freedom of conscience* claims. 'Strasbourg' argued that while freedom of religion may generally be exercised by a corporate entity, freedom of conscience is 'by [its] very nature not susceptible of [*sic*] being exercised by a legal person'.[25]

5. The Court's 1990s and 2000s case law offers some perspective for corporate religious freedom, albeit requiring a rather benevolent reading. First, in a case brought by *inter alia* a publishing company of the Finnish Freethinkers once again challenging a church tax regime – benefitting the two national churches of Finland (Lutheran and Orthodox) – standing was denied on account of this applicant being an LLC. Specifically, it concluded that '*in the circumstances of the present case* the applicant company cannot rely on' religious freedom.[26] Quite a lot can be read into that disclaimer since the Commission held it as crucial that the applicant had not proven that the Freethinkers *Association* (a separate applicant, founded to promote separation of state and national churches in Finland) 'would have been prevented

---

25 E.g. *Verein 'Kontakt-Information-Therapie' (KIT) and Siegfried Hagen v. Austria*, No. 11921/86, decision of 12 October 1988; reiterated with respect to other aspects of religious (and other) rights in ECommHR, *Scientology Kirche Deutchland e.V. v. Germany*, No. 34614/97, decision of 7 April 1997, The Law.

26 *Kustannus Oy Vapaa Ajattelija AB, Vapaa-Ajattelijain Liitto - Fritänkarnas Förbund r.y. and Kimmo Sundström v. Finland*, No. 20471/92, decision of 15 April 1996 (emphasis added).

from pursuing the company's commercial activities in its own name'. In other words, a corporate entity not being quite as corporate as an LLC and having some but not exclusive commercial objects probably qualifies as rights-holder under the Convention and probably its commercial activities, too, would fall within the scope of the religious freedom clause. Those are a lot of 'probablies', but essentially that reading is confirmed in the most recent case law. A French Jewish syndicate that was incorporated as a 'liturgical' association to, among other objectives, represent the interests of ritual slaughterers, but which in actual fact also employed both kashrut inspectors and commercial ritual slaughterers and imported *glatt* kosher meat from Belgium, i.e. that was very much active in both the commercial and the religious department, could as a corporate entity rely on freedom of religion or belief according to the Grand Chamber of the European Court of Human Rights.[27] This is the nearest the Court has come to embracing corporate religious freedom.

3.2   CORPORATE RELIGIOUS FREEDOM: THE ARGUMENTS FOR AND AGAINST

Accordingly, international monitoring bodies are more or less reluctantly coming to terms with the possibility of a corporate legal entity exercising religious freedom. Especially where commercial motives are prominent on the part of the incorporated entity, the reluctance to accept the applicability of collective religious freedom has been significant. The principal and principled arguments against corporate religious freedom are profound.

---

27   *Cha'are Shalom Ve Tsedek v. France*, No. 27417/95, 27 June 2000, para. 74. A split decision with dissent by seven judges; note that the association did not go on to win its case.

A first, ontological argument insists that companies cannot 'be' religious.[28] Attributing religion, and hence religious freedom claims, inevitably requires human agency; hence, rights discourse would do well to keep the focus on the individual, not the collective. A second argument is more normative and points to the Pandora's box of unbridled corporate religious freedom which may be vast and vastly damaging, potentially causing a myriad of corporate claims for exemptions, special treatment, and other privileges, fostering unchecked tax evasion by unscrupulous business churches that, while they are at it, cajole impressionable religionists out of their hard-won savings, and so forth.

Yet whether categorically dismissing corporate religious freedom is viable or even desirable may be questioned. A number of ontological, public diplomacy and legal theory arguments can be identified in support of the notion of corporate religious freedom:

1. *Necessity of restrictions:* A first 'argument for' simply seeks to refute the chief 'argument against'. Indeed, should said doom scenario – Pandora's box – materialize there is certainly ample reason for concern; yet unsubstantiated fear per se does not justify human rights restrictions or the denial of rights altogether. The a priori denial of corporate religious freedom based on the potentially adverse effects of that freedom-as-unbridled-freedom ignores the inherent checks and balances of the human rights system, notably the fact that the rights of others are expressly recognized internationally as potential limiting factors.

---

28 E.g. generally, Ginsburg's dissent in *Hobby Lobby*; Robert Parry, 'The Right's Misconstrued Constitution', *Consortiumnews* (29 November 13).

2. *State practice:* While not remotely amounting to custom, increasingly state practice is characterized by laws or case law embracing – vastly differing – notions of corporate religious freedom.[29] The relative ease with which domestic judiciaries (and occasionally legislators) broaden the scope of religious ownership of rights so as to include companies, as compared to international monitoring bodies, presumably has to do with the fact that the terms of reference with which the latter bodies work are traditionally more rigidly preoccupied with the philosophy of *individual* religious freedoms. Then, this is only a partial explanation and not a wholly satisfactory one given that many other internationally recognized human rights have been declared applicable to collective legal entities. Hence, it seems as though international monitoring bodies are wary of the legal ramifications of an inclusive reading of collective religious freedom in and of itself.

3. *Religious-commercial activities:* This argument pro engages with the ontological argument against. Essentially, the argument holds, disqualifying commercial activity from the scope of religious freedom protection is inexplicable and

---

29 States endorsing corporate religious freedom in their law or case law include: USA (US Supreme Court, *Hobby Lobby* judgment 2014); Germany (Constitutional Court, 2 BVR 208/76, 25 March 1980), while Swiss, French, Spanish and Italian courts have also ruled that companies with a religious ethos can exercise certain religious rights. These decisions have involved children daycare centres, private universities, media outlets and private hospitals. *Mutatis mutandis*, the EU also promotes the religious autonomy of private organizations with a for-profit motive that are based on a religious or philosophical ethos by way of exempting these from certain EU equal employment opportunities regulation. See Art. 4 of Council Directive 2000/78/EC of 27 November 2000 establishing a general framework for equal treatment in employment and occupation. For other examples of state practice, see Elizabeth Clark and Cole Durham, 'The Emergence of Corporate Religious Freedom', in M. Evans et al. (eds.), *Changing Nature of Religious Rights under International Law* (Oxford: OUP, 2015, pp. 268-273, providing details regarding among other states Argentina, UK, and Spain.

ignores reality. Take religious butchers: ritual slaughter is at one and the same time a deeply religious activity and a commercial activity. The religious butcher ensures the religious dietary needs of the flock, yet the ritual slaughterer's adage is also: 'There's no such thing as a free lunch'. The same goes for religious banks, religious publishing, and countless other activities: they serve religious needs and (may) make money at the same time. From the perspective of legal theory it is not clear why religious freedom protection should cease once a for-profit motive has been established. True, fraudulent 'business churches' may abuse their incorporated status to dodge taxes and other generally applicable laws, but this does not detract from the fact that there exists a category of genuine religious-commercial activities. Moreover, tax evasion, fraud and other malpractice can be dealt with under the generic tax and criminal laws in place, and since religious freedom allows for public order limitations in any event, narrowing the very scope of religious freedom a priori may be unwarranted.

4. *Corporate conscience:* Commercial activity not – to the layman – neatly inspired by or inextricably linked with religious practices or obligations may nonetheless derive protection from religious freedom by dint of the *freedom of conscience* aspect of this right. Indeed, the distinction made in international case law between a protectable generic corporate religious freedom and an unprotected corporate conscience is problematic.[30] Both alternative extremes are stronger. The one extreme, namely that there can be nothing of the sort – no religion and no conscience – on the part of a corporation

---

30 Cf. ECtHR case law, e.g. *Verein 'Kontakt-Information-Therapie' (KIT) and Siegfried Hagen v. Austria* and *Scientology Kirche Deutchland e.V. v. Germany.*

is certainly defensible (though, I expect, belied by law and case law, both domestically and internationally). After all, the reason underlying some forms of incorporation (including LLCs) is to create an artificial but legally very significant distinction between a person and a company. Therefore, the coincidence of company and personal conscience does make more sense in the case of sole proprietorship and other small unincorporated businesses. That said, incorporated businesses can in practice be *closely held*, that is, owned by a relatively small and constant shareholder base, which consequently is in a position to put its religious mark on the enterprise. With respect to such sole proprietor, family-owned, or otherwise closely-held companies, it stands to reason then (and this is the second alternative extreme) that the legal representation metaphor underlies the attribution of religion to a corporation as much as it does the attribution of conscience. Obviously, no company is 'religious' in the literal sense of possessing cognition; the same goes for conscience. But once we accept that a corporate entity is legally equipped to represent its owners and their collective religious freedom claims, isolating and disqualifying 'conscience' from the legal proxy act is inexplicable. This argument is further supported by other legal fictions pertaining to corporate entities, e.g. their being held criminally liable based on corporate criminal intent.[31] Indeed, under vast sections of corporate, criminal, and tax law the attribution of intentions to corporate entities is unexceptional.[32]

---

31 Amy J. Sepinwall, 'Corporate Piety and Impropriety', 5 *Harvard Business Law Review* (2015), at pp. 183-190.

32 E.g. Howard Kislowicz, 'Business Corporations as Religious Freedom Claimants in Canada', *SSRN* (2017).

5. *International law and the corporate conscience:* Barring corporate conscience from the scope of religious freedom is not only inexplicable, it is also hypocritical. The international community constantly attributes conscience to companies. If anything, the UN, OSCE, OESO, EU, etc. want more rather than less conscience on the part of corporations. Nike is spurred on to stop using child labour, McDonalds is called upon not to deforest the world, Shell is prompted not to spill more oil, and so on.[33] Any argument that companies may only have consciences that come in handy from the perspective of the values promoted by international law, such as corporate social responsibility and other progressive values, but not conservative consciences or consciences informed by metaphysical ethics, is untenable.

6. *Public diplomacy:* Perhaps the most important argument is that any stated or unstated concerns in this debate, i.e. those public goods at stake like the fundamental *rights of others*, which are ostensibly protected by obstinately denying the very notion of corporate religious freedom, are in actual fact best spelled out in a transparent and fair evaluation of such colliding rights cases by engaging with those concerns about the rights of others whilst considering the merits of the collective religious freedom complaint.

Spelling out those opposing concerns in a transparent and fair fashion is what I will embark upon now.

---

33 See also Clark and Durham, *supra* note 29.

4. CORPORATE RELIGIOUS FREEDOM'S INTERPLAY WITH OTHER HUMAN RIGHTS: AN INVENTORY OF TENSION

At the domestic level, recently and increasingly private commercial enterprises have claimed religious freedom violations. Whether successful or not, what all these claim have in common is that a collective religious conscience is attributed to the corporate entity. What these claims typically also have in common is that the conscience of the company, and by association the religious autonomy of the belief community represented by the corporate entity, is threatened by generally applicable laws, unless special 'accommodation' is made for the company to permit the action or inaction dictated by religion. What these claims still further have in common is that typically fundamental *rights of others* are affected if and to the extent the legal accommodation is granted. A brief, non-exhaustive overview:

Women's rights, notably women's reproductive rights, have been engaged by corporate religious freedom claims. The traditional examples of pharmacies and doctors, including those employed by private for-profit healthcare corporations, conscientiously objecting to contraceptives, abortifacients, or indeed abortions, are well known and subject to a vast body of case law and scholarship. The *Hobby Lobby* judgment of the US Supreme Court illustrates that similar issues extend to business enterprises beyond the realm of healthcare per se.[34] Hobby Lobby, a chain of arts and crafts shops with over 800 stores and some

---

34   US Supreme Court, *Burwell v. Hobby Lobby*, 573 U.S. (2014).

32,000 employees, objected to what is known in the US as the 'contraceptive mandate', a scheme by which private employers are obliged to cover contraceptive costs for their female employees. Specifically, the company's owners believed that four out of the 20 contraceptives covered through the scheme were in fact abortifacients (since those have the effect of preventing the fertilized egg from developing and attaching to the uterus), which is contrary to the dictates of their religion. The US Supreme Court ruled that Hobby Lobby's religious liberty was breached and struck down part of the contraceptive mandate. Accordingly, while non-accommodation of the company's religious objection to the contraceptive mandate could have substantially burdened the free exercise of religion by the company's owners, the religious freedom accommodation that was made undermines Obamacare's central tenet of *affordable* care and women's full control over their reproductive lives.

Second, *LGBT rights* might be engaged by corporate religious freedom claims. This category no longer exclusively pertains to scant instances involving family hotels refusing homosexual customers in non-urban areas. The proliferation of corporate freedom claims can be explained by dint of certain societal and historical developments. First and foremost is the emancipation of LGBTs as such. The instant conflict could necessarily only first emerge in pluralist societies where LGBTs enjoy basic rights and can openly manifest their sexual orientation and openly seek access to public and private services. Conscientious objections in, for example, the medical sphere, were debated long before homosexuality lost some of its taboo status. Thus, whereas intolerance vis-à-vis sexual minorities as such has existed since time immemorial, these conscientious objections are relatively novel – they simply did not need to be voiced in the employment or service sectors because the latter were typically not visibly faced with applications from LGBTs. As LGBTs within western societies become more emancipated and vocal, the ante is upped beyond mere legal toleration, and instead towards promoting substantive equality in all areas of public and private life, which includes securing equal employment opportunities and equal treatment. At the same time, religion-based corporations are formulating religious objections to advancing gay rights couched in religious freedom terminology. As a result, a wide range of modern generally applicable laws is being challenged, including equal treatment laws. The instant clash typically manifests itself as a refusal to provide services: a private business enterprise refusing its services to a client on account of the sexual orientation of the latter. While such refusals first emerged within the wedding services trade[35] – i.e. florists, bakeries, photographers, caterers, etc., in those states that recognize same-sex marriage – and initially also particularly affected commercial goods or services characterized by an express 'gay pride' signature,[36] service refusals may affect private services across the board. This is illustrated by the fact that a private university in Canada, Trinity Western University, pleaded religious freedom to justify its policy of discouraging LGBTs from enrolling. While non-accommodation of the religious freedom claim might interfere with the conscience rights of these business owners, permitting these service refusals amounts to sanctioning direct discrimination on grounds of sexual orientation.

---

35 E.g. US Supreme Court, *Masterpiece Cakeshop v. Colorado Civil Rights Commission*, 584 U.S. (2018).

36 E.g. UK Supreme Court, *Lee v. Ashers Baking Company Ltd and others*, 18 October 2018 ('Gay Cake Case', concerning a cake with pro-gay marriage message); Dutch Equal Rights Commission, Case No. 2010-32, 9 March 2010 (concerning the refusal of a company to print a text on towels for a pro-LGBT rights event).

Naturally, corporate religious freedom claims might also engage the *religious freedom rights of others*. Corporate religious entities may not only wish to insulate themselves from 'the sinful' and from regulations that run counter to their corporate conscience, the religion-based company may also more generally aspire to keeping the workplace religiously homogeneous. This typically affects employment opportunities. In contrast to LGBT-related refusals, it is less a question of access to the business product or rendered service as such. A number of categories can be analytically distinguished. First a corporate entity with a religious ethos may seek to bar employment of persons adhering to *other* religions and beliefs, or indeed those who have no religion.[37] Second, a religious company may seek to uphold that religious ethos in the face of members of that *same religion* who, in the view of the company, practise the tenets of that religion insufficiently, inadequately or otherwise display behaviour deemed at odds with the company's religious ethos.[38] Both these scenarios lead to a standoff between freedoms of religion.

Another sub-category here is provided by *freedom from religion* claims by secular companies. Whereas some companies may want to create a religiously homogeneous workplace, have a religious ethos influence corporate decisions and work ethics, recruitment strategies and customer service, other companies

---

37　E.g., *mutatis mutandis*, Dutch Human Rights Commission, Case No. 2015-68, 9 June 2015, concerning Salvation Army's refusal to hire a non-religious HR person; Dutch Human Rights Commission, Case No. 2011-141, 22 September 2012.

38　E.g., ECtHR, *Fernández Martínez v. Spain*, Application No. 56030/07, 12 June 2014; *Siebenhaar v. Germany*, Application No. 18136/02, 3 February 2011; UN Human Rights Committee, *William Eduardo Delgado Páez v. Colombia*, Communication No. 195/1985, 12 July 1990. US Supreme Court, *Hosanna-Tabor Evangelical Lutheran Church and School v. Equal Employment Opportunity Commission*, 565 U.S. 171 (2012).

might want to keep religion out. While there are few examples of corporate enterprises *expressly* being based on an atheist, agnostic, or humanist ethos, quite a few companies are by default secular because they do not have a religious mission statement. This has led to scenarios in which companies have attempted to ban 'ostentatious' manifestations of religion, like religious dress or symbols.[39] In practice the legal argument tends not to rely on corporate freedom from religion so much as on the freedom of association and especially organizational autonomy, i.e. entrepreneurial freedom, or in EU jargon, the 'freedom to conduct a business'. A secular company's entrepreneurial freedom may also join forces with equal rights, notably pro-LGBT rights policies, leading to the possibility of disciplinary measures being taken against those staff who unilaterally refuse to serve LGBTs.[40] This, too, is an example of a clash between aggregated corporate freedoms versus the conscientious rights of the individual employee.

The uniting factor in all these categories is the claim that non-accommodation of the religious freedom claim would lead to undue interferences with religious or secular ethos-driven entrepreneurial freedom.

---

39 ECtHR, *Eweida and Others v. UK*, Application Nos. 48420/10, 59842/10, 51671/10 and 36516/10, 15 January 2013; CJEU, *Achbita v. G4S Secure Solutions NV*, Judgment of the Court (Grand Chamber) of 14 March 2017; Cour de Cassation (Assemblée Plénière), *Baby Loup* case, Arrêt nº 612, 25 June 2014.
40 E.g. the *McFarlane* case (see *Eweida ibid.*).

5. ASSESSING PLURALIST CONFLICTS INVOLVING CORPORATE RELIGIOUS FREEDOM

5.1 JUDGING PLURALIST CONFLICTS: GENERAL CONTOURS

From the examples we have seen that complete accommodation of the corporate religious freedom claim, typically in the form of an exemption from a generally applicable law, is bound to interfere with the rights of others; whereas complete non-accommodation of the corporate conscience claim – if collective religious freedom is accepted as a legal notion – is bound to interfere with corporate religious freedom, notably religious autonomy and entrepreneurial freedom. When it comes to judging such pluralist rights conflicts, the first and foremost baseline is that competing rights in principle are recognized by international human rights law, whether it is collective religious freedom on the one hand and, for instance, women's rights or LGBT rights on the other. Also, there exists no a priori hierarchy of fundamental rights under international law. Furthermore, the right to freedom of religion or belief – like a number of other fundamental rights – is not an absolute right. Specifically, while no state interference whatsoever with the core freedom to have or adopt or change one's religion – the *forum internum* – is permitted, the freedom to manifest a religion or belief – the *forum externum* – is subject to such limitations as are prescribed by law and are necessary to protect 'public safety, order, health, or morals or the fundamental rights and freedoms of others'.[41]

---

41   ICCPR, Art. 18(3). ECHR, Art. 9 lists similar grounds for restriction.

In order to come to equitable solutions, existing tests, models or guidelines for assessing the present type of human rights conflicts place tremendous emphasis on the need to measure, as precisely as possible, the interference with religious freedom should accommodation not be made.[42] To some extent that is only logical, since most such models, guidelines and human rights tests are first and foremost developed based on domestic legal discourses and on the cases brought to (domestic) courts to date.[43] My list of guidelines is largely premised on shifting the centre of gravity of the human rights assessment to the flip-side (or at least emphasizing this flip-side throughout the human rights analysis): i.e. charting the harm done to third parties should the accommodation of religious freedom be made and the reasonableness or unreasonableness of that hardship whilst generally assuming that non-accommodation interferes with religious freedom. Establishing a religious freedom interference, it is contended, is but part of the puzzle; it is the interplay with the rights of others that answers pivotal (international human rights test-oriented) questions of necessity and proportionality. An additional benefit is that, whereas secular authorities, including the judiciary, are ill-positioned to minutely measure religious hardship (the severity of the interference is after all

---

42   Resulting in such factors as 'severity' and 'directness'. See e.g. Cécile Laborde, 'Egalitarian Justice and Religious Exemptions', in Susanna Mancini and Michel Rosenfeld (eds.), *The Conscience Wars: Rethinking the Balance between Religion, Identity and Equality* (Cambridge: CUP, 2018), p. 114-116; Eva Brems, 'Objections to Antidiscrimination in the Name of Conscience or Religion', in *ibid.*, pp. 284-285 ('Criteria for Prioritization', likewise including 'severity').

43   E.g. establishing with some degree of preciseness the severity of the 'burden' on religious liberty is particularly legally relevant within US legal doctrine.

conscience dependent),[44] the harm that may befall third parties can be established more or less objectively.

My first set of principles (A) affect the area of recruitment and human resources *sensu latu* (including dismissals/demotions, access to work-related benefits):

A1. *Direct versus indirect discrimination:* Those who seek employment with a company but are rejected on grounds of religion or other characteristics the company opposes for religious reasons face direct discrimination: looking at the discrimination spectrum, harm does not get much more severe than such forms of in-your-face discrimination.[45] When it comes to the religiously motivated impact of the corporate conscience *during* employment, we may occasionally detect instances of more indirect types of discrimination and harm (which, it should be noted, must also be accompanied by a reasonable and objective justification under international law for it to be legitimate). For instance, Hobby Lobby presumably does not deny contraceptives to women because they are women, but because the company opposes the very federal contraceptive mandate, something which in turn affects women's reproductive healthcare rights.

A1(a). *Recruitment:* Differential treatment during recruitment would nearly always amount to direct discrimination and hence be prohibited under international law and normally under domestic law too. One exception is those jobs where religion specifically

---

44   As acknowledged by Laborde, *ibid.*, p. 114.

45   That said, 'dignitarian harm' as outlined below under B.3 may amount to intense hardship too (some may even argue more intense, on account of the state's complicity with such harm), even when it is not of an in-your-face nature.

is a *genuine and determining occupational requirement*, but in the corporate world, i.e. outside the realm of churches and not-for-profit religious organizations, such positions would be very scarce indeed. There is debate as to whether private organizations or companies expressly based on a 'religious ethos' should get more licence for making distinctions within their recruitment policies so as to make the workplace wholly religiously homogeneous, affecting such positions for which religion is not a determining occupational requirement (cleaning personnel, canteen staff, etc.). I would argue this is overstepping the mark and provides too large a licence to discriminate. At the risk of entering religious doctrinal debate, it may be questioned whether *corporate* religious autonomy truly requires the possibility of complete religious homogeneity. Taken to its extreme, that position would also mean that each company that establishes itself on a secular/atheist/humanist/agnostic/etc. ethos would acquire a licence to bar each and every job application from religious persons. Notwithstanding such concerns, EU's Equal Treatment Framework Directive has paved the way towards such a comprehensive exception to equal treatment by immunizing 'private organizations the ethos of which is based on religion or belief' from charges of discrimination.[46] Such distinctions made by religious ethos organizations, however, 'should not justify discrimination on another ground',[47] which blocks the possibility of discriminating e.g. LGBTs in recruitment processes.

---

46 Council Directive 2000/78/EC of 27 November 2000 establishing a general framework for equal treatment in employment and occupation, Art. 4(2), omitting the word 'determining'.

47 *Ibid.*

A1(b). *Conflicts during employment:* That religious communities, generally speaking, should be reasonably accommodated so that they can uphold their religious ethos in an autonomous fashion is relatively uncontested – even if this means that the legal entitlements of individual members of that religion may get sidelined. A series of landmark judgments, both at the international level and domestically, have confirmed that 'religious exemptions' or 'ministerial exceptions' (US) may apply to religious communities, immunizing them from aspects of equal treatment laws. The European Court of Human Rights, in a series of judgments prioritizing religious autonomy, sanctioned disciplinary measures, including the dismissal of an adulterous Mormon public relations officer (yet similar measures as a result of the extramarital escapades of a Catholic organist were deemed irregular),[48] and vis-à-vis married and 'atheist priests'.[49] The UN Human Rights Committee, too, prioritized religious autonomy in cases involving religious loyalty conflicts between employer and employee, for instance, in a case concerning the unauthorized teaching of liberation theology at Catholic schools.[50] Similarly, in *Hosanna-Tabor* the US Supreme Court applied the ministerial exception for the first time – in a unanimous ruling – to a loyalty conflict between an employee and a private Lutheran school, to the advantage of the religious autonomy of the latter.[51] Belonging to a different religious community per se can also make one 'disloyal' in the eyes of religious employers. Accordingly, a Protestant day-care centre felt that

---

48 *Obst v. Germany*, No. 425/03, 23 September 2010; cf. *Schüth v. Germany*, No. 1620/03, 23 September 2010.
49 *Fernández Martínez v. Spain*, No. 56030/07, 12 June 2014 (GC).
50 *William Eduardo Delgado Páez v. Colombia*, Communication No. 195/1985, 12 July 1990, para. 5.9.
51 *Hosanna-Tabor* judgment (2012).

active membership of the Universal Church was at odds with its ethos and fired the employee concerned without notice, something upheld by the European Court of Human Rights.[52] In sum, a significant degree religious autonomy in loyalty conflict cases appears jurisprudentially fairly well entrenched. Nevertheless, I would like to add some additional considerations – in the form of prioritization principles – in this regard.

A2. *Foreseeability:* What is significant in such loyalty conflicts is the fact that individuals voluntarily acceded a faith community and its religious ethos, and the concomitant fact that the adverse consequences as a result of non-compliance with the said ethos are to some extent foreseeable. While assuming lower hardship for 'insiders' due to 'foreseeability' generally stands to reason, this notion does beg two obvious questions: (i) What can be deemed 'foreseeable'? And (ii) who can be deemed 'insiders'?[53] As for foreseeability, the question here is whether religious authorities, and religious *employers* in particular, have absolute discretion when it comes to determining what constitute disloyal acts and what may be the ramifications of disloyal behaviour. The cases of adulterous or religiously non-practising employees mentioned previously are the 'easy cases' in that respect. One will appreciate the tension here between risking the 'slippery slope' of ever-more demanding loyalty requirements, abuse of autonomy, and unreasonable insistence on absolute religious homogeneity, far beyond the realm of genuine occupational requirements and due protection of the corporate religious ethos *versus* monitoring bodies second-guessing corporate qualifications as

---

52 *Siebenhaar v. Germany*, No. 18136/02, 3 February 2011.
53 And (iii), how about the fact that religious affiliation might change over time, or the fact that someone might come out of the closet in the course of one's employment, and so on? These variables are beyond the scope of this account.

to loyalty, thus inevitably encroaching on religious autonomy. The 'insiders' label, too, can be tricky and unduly disempower vulnerable members of the in-crowd. So yes, Mr Obst, the Mormon public affairs officer, knew he was skating on thin ice when he embarked on his extramarital escapades; and arguably Mrs Siebenhaar should have known that her allegiances with the Universal Church were offensive to her employer, while Mr Paez should have been aware that the ecclesiastical authorities and the Vatican in particular are no great fans of liberation theology (though Francis is less anti than Ratzinger). But how far does the concept of 'insiders' stretch? For instance, can the female workers of Hobby Lobby actually be considered to have knowingly and voluntarily joined a faith community by taking up their employment with this sizable chain of art and craft shops and thereby willingly waived some of their women's rights to health? This seems unlikely. These concerns about the concepts of insiders and foreseeability mean that religious exemptions can ultimately only be contemplated with respect to *closely-held* companies that are, moreover, *transparent* about the religious ethos of the company and the ramifications thereof during recruitment processes. The argument cuts both ways: only then can a case for hardship on the part of the owners be truly made and only then does the analogy with a faith community stand; while reversely, only then can the fall-out (whether this consists of the loss of jobs, demotions, non-access to otherwise available benefits, etc.) be contained, should the accommodation be made.

A3. *Legitimate Aims and Necessity:* What makes the current type of human rights assessment so convoluted is the fact that it is within a *horizontal relationship between two non-state actors* that we are ascertaining whether the state's actions or inactions – intended to preserve the rights of one party but thereby potentially interfering with the rights of another rights-holder – could be deemed 'necessary' in a democratic society. Against that backdrop, the recent advance of the neutrality principle, well into the territory of private, horizontal settings is striking – and legally troublesome. Specifically, the Court of Justice of the EU has considered it legitimate for a secular company to invoke neutrality – such a policy choice may be distilled from 'the freedom to conduct a business' – in order to discipline or ultimately fire employees who display their personal religious convictions through their religious attire.[54] The concern here is not that secular companies enjoy religious freedom including, in its negative modality, freedom *from* religion. This goes without saying. After all, freedom of religion or belief under international law is broadly construed and protects 'theistic, non-theistic and atheistic beliefs, as well as the right not to profess any religion or belief'.[55] Thus, if religious ethos companies benefit from corporate religious freedom then so do secular companies. What is concerning is that neutrality is accepted within private, horizontal relations as a legitimate aim to restrict individual rights and that the necessity of neutrality within the corporate world is taken for granted. As the Luxembourg Court puts it, 'the fact that workers are prohibited from visibly wearing signs of political, philosophical or religious beliefs is appropriate for the purpose of ensuring that a policy of neutrality is properly applied...'.[56] Is it though? Is it self-evident that eradicating religious symbols is a necessary means towards preserving neutrality? Do individual religious manifestations adversely affect the company's image

---

54　*Achbita v. G4S Secure Solutions NV*, Judgment of the Court (Grand Chamber) of 14 March 2017.

55　UN Human Rights Committee, General Comment 22: Article 18 (1993), para. 2.

56　*Achbita v. G4S Secure Solutions NV*, para. 40.

and are companies only right to take measures against any such negative branding? Is neutrality achieved by acts of exclusion and securing homogeneity, or is neutrality actually premised on pluralism? In a pluralist society comfortable with its pluralism an individual displaying religious attire would not be perceived as harmful or offensive either by the company or by the customers. A company where personnel can openly allude to the various religions present in society, or indeed a company actually accommodating the various religious freedom needs of its versatile workforce, could be deemed very much neutral if 'neutrality' is less poorly defined.[57] On top of all that, the judgment by the EU Court of Justice has caused international law to be fragmented on this point, since its Strasbourg colleague – the European Court of Human Rights – ruled in a similar case concerning an airline company that '[t]here was no evidence that the wearing of other, previously authorized, items of religious clothing, such as turbans and hijabs, by other employees, had any negative impact on British Airways' brand or image'.[58] Consequently, while an 'employer's wish to project a certain corporate image'[59] may be a legitimate aim to limit fundamental rights, there is still a significant burden of proof to be met to actually establish that religious dress or symbols are detrimental to the company's brand. The same goes for other arguments companies advance with a view to legitimizing religious dress bans, such as the fear of proselytism or the emancipation of women, interests that are

---

57 For more inclusive conceptualizations of liberal neutrality, see e.g. Roland Pierik and Wibren van der Burg, 'What is Neutrality', *Amsterdam Law School Research Paper* (No. 2011-20), proposing 'inclusive proportional neutrality'; and Jeroen Temperman, *State–Religion Relationships and Human Rights Law* (Leiden/Boston: Brill/Martinus Nijhoff Publishers, 2010), developing (a right to) 'religiously neutral governance'.

58 *Eweida and Others v. the United*, para. 94.

59 *Ibid.*

typically advanced within employment sectors like childcare or education.[60] Adopted under a cloak of corporate social responsibility, such policies actually undermine women rights, while the need for such horizontal neutrality policing is at best debatable.

A4. *Less interfering alternatives:* Proportionality also and especially refers to the need to ascertain, prior to altogether sacrificing one right in favour of another human rights or public order principle, whether less interfering alternatives are imaginable that, if not optimally, better respect the rights under consideration. Within the human resources context, one such alternative could be for companies to offer the employee an alternative position. That is, some religion-based loyalty or labour conflicts would not need to lead to outright dismissals, thus protecting – to some extent – the rights of others (here employees) and protecting – to some extent – the religious autonomy of the corporation, after all the company's wish to remove the employee from the position at stake is granted. Conflicts that have an important financial aspect to them can – in theory at least – often be mitigated by way of reallocating the costs incurred. If, from a national point of view, these costs are 'negligible or reasonable'[61] such costs shifting (typically to the state/general public) could be precisely what religious freedom requires. In essence, this means granting full religious accommodation while simultaneously ensuring that whatever public good risks getting eradicated by the accommodation is salvaged through additional state action. Exactly what is reasonable and what not is, however, far from crystallized. For instance, the net result of granting Hobby Lobby an exemption from the contraceptive mandate is that the

---

60 These corporate interests were advanced e.g. in the French *Baby Loup* case. Cour de Cassation (Assemblée Plénière), Arrêt n° 612, 25 June 2014.
61 Laborde, *supra* note 39, p. 118.

'general public can pick up the tab'.[62] Also, what is negligible now may not be in the future, especially considering that these judgments provide a precedent to opt out of generally applicable laws, in this case healthcare laws affecting women's reproductive rights.

My second set of prioritization guiding principles affects the service side of religious ethos companies:

B1. *Service-based versus person-based rejections:* Entering the external, worldly side of companies' operations means that equal access and equal treatment principles vis-à-vis third parties seeking the company's services are engaged. While equality norms affect the internal realm of recruitment too, at the service end of the business there can be no question of foreseeability, voluntariness or insider status: under equal treatment laws, everyone is entitled to equal access to both public and private services offered on the market to the general public.[63] There are other considerations that help demarcate the room for manoeuvre in this area. Assessing conscientious objections, it is meaningful to distinguish between *service-based rejections* and *person-based rejections*, as this enables us to qualify the degree of direct harm suffered. To be sure, all persons who seeks a company's service but who are rejected on account of a religion-based

---

62   Justice Ginsburg's dissent in *Hobby Lobby*.
63   Cf. e.g. UK Supreme Court in *Bull v. Hall*, [2013] UKSC 37, at 51, emphasizing that 'the protection of the rights and freedoms of [the same-sex couple] provided a reason to reject the sought-after exemption from antidiscrimination law' in a case in which hotel owners had refused a room to a gay couple (as they refused to 'facilitate' their 'sinful' lifestyles).

objection to one – or more[64] – of their characteristics (be it the latter's dissimilar religion, or sexual orientation, and/or gender) face direct discrimination, yet the rejection experienced can be placed along a spectrum of being more or less 'personal'. In that respect, it should be noted that the contemporary conscientious objections emerging in the era of conscience wars, as compared to the traditional objections raised in medical contexts, differ analytically in one crucial respect: those pharmacists and doctors who fundamentally and for religious reasons object to performing the requested service or action object to the very service or action at stake – indeed, presumably they would not even wish to avail of it themselves. Modern-day businesses whose services are sought by LGBTs, whether they are wedding photographers, bakers, caterers, educators, and so on, do not object to the service that is sought from them – indeed, this service is their core business, they render it day after day. They object to a human trait of the customer or at least the latter's decision to openly manifest this trait. All in all, this means that we are not only facing direct harm caused by direct discrimination on grounds of sexual orientation, but that direct harm is moreover very much targeted at the very person of the one being rejected. The argument that this scenario would also amount to a service rejection, as the religionist in question would not necessarily have anything against the targeted LGBT, but merely against being implicated in his or her lifestyle through 'being forced' to serve him or her, is not convincing.[65] In fact, the argument is

---

64 The hardship in case of 'intersectional' discrimination tends to be especially insidious and hence may cause aggravated hardship. On intersectionality, see e.g. Kimberlé Crenshaw, 'Mapping the Margins: Intersectionality, Identity Politics, and Violence against Women of Color' (1991) 46:6 *Stanford Law Review* 1241-1299.

65 E.g. Andrew Koppelman, 'You Can't Hurry Love: Why Antidiscrimination Protections for Gay People Should Have Religious Exemptions', 72 *Brooklyn Law Review* (2006), p. 135 (referring to 'forced associations with gay people').

rather disingenuous. Let us call a spade a spade. I do not see any difference between a sign in a shop effectively saying 'Jews not welcome', or 'Blacks not welcome', and one that says 'Gays not welcome'. The underlying reasoning also hardly seems to matter. Whether theories of racial superiority or religiously motivated homophobia inspire the rejection, in all cases the rejection boils down to an act of intolerance vis-à-vis a person based on personal traits. The next customer who enters the shop and who is not gay is served; that is what matters.

B2. *Complicity, conscience and communication:* On the service side occasionally models and guidelines attempt to quantify the harm of non-accommodation of the religious conscience claim using a notion of 'complicity'.[66] The more complicit in the act the conscientious objector is, the more hardship is incurred and the stronger the appeal to allow the religious accommodation. Recommendations made can be as specific as singling out for instance wedding photography, which would make the photographer opposed to same-sex marriage particularly complicit inasmuch as such photography 'is considered an integral part of the [marriage] affirmation'.[67] Again I think it best if secular judges steer clear of religious doctrinal debates and the question of the exact impact on conscience. Generally, again, the interference with religious freedom can be assumed and the focus is best shifted to the impact on the rights of others if the accommodation is made. That said, something of a *sui generis* category is perhaps provided by the scenario where the client seeks a product with an express pro-gay (rights) message, such as materials

---

66 See e.g., generally, Douglas NeJaime and Reva B. Siegel, *supra* note 1.

67 Michael Rosenfeld, 'The Conscience Wars in Historical and Philosophical Perspective', in Susanna Mancini and Michel Rosenfeld (eds.), *The Conscience Wars: Rethinking the Balance between Religion, Identity and Equality* (Cambridge: CUP, 2018), p. 87.

for gay pride events. This does potentially and rather objectively increase the objectionable nature of rendering the product/service at stake to those with conscientious objections. Whether it is enough to outweigh equal treatment rights is to be decided on a case by case basis, but in any event domestic case law would do well to relate pro-conscientious objection arguments to the conscientiously objectionable nature of the product/service sought and the nature of the refusal, and to the way in which the rejection is communicated (see also under B.3),[68] and not to the qualities of the client seeking it, even though the line will be extremely fine in these situations. The recent British 'Gay Cake' case serves as an example. In permitting the refusal of the order for a cake on which the words 'Support Gay Marriage' needed to be iced, the UK Supreme Court emphasized that the born-again Christian shop owners opposed the message, not necessarily the customer.[69]

B3. *Direct and expressive harm:* Person-based rejections foster *direct harm* on the part of the person rejected: the person is not rendered a service on account of who s/he is. Both the immediate denial – even if only temporary – of access to the service at stake as well as experienced feelings of rejection, insult, or anguish, are part of the direct harm suffered on account of a

---

68 In fact, communication can be key also and especially if 'complicity' is *not* emphasized in the rejection. A private company is certainly entitled in most jurisdictions to refuse orders on neutral grounds, if they are genuine and consistently applied (e.g. 'We do not cater for weddings'). See also Rosenfeld, *ibid.*, p. 87; Lorenzo Zucca, 'Is There a Right to Conscientious Objection?', in *ibid.*, p. 146.

69 UK Supreme Court, *Lee v. Ashers Baking Company Ltd and others*, 18 October 2018, para. 55.

service denial.[70] Moreover, the rejectee may also suffer *expressive harm*. 'Expressive harm' is suffered by someone when s/he 'is treated according to principles that express negative or inappropriate attitudes toward' her or him.[71] Expressive harm is harm done to the dignity of persons – 'dignity harm' or 'dignitarian harm'[72] – and is caused by scenarios wherein the state is, as it were, implicated in the act of rejection. Direct harm is caused by the rejection; expressive harm is caused or exacerbated by the law (or policy, or judgment, or otherwise the actions, inactions or attitudes of public authorities).[73] These dynamics occur where the state has taken a priori measures in favour of religious exemptions to equal treatment law. As a result of those measures, the rejectee feels that s/he has been ill-treated not only by the intolerant person who rejects him or her, but feels ill-treated too by the state (authorities) for not only not taking measures against the act of discrimination but actually facilitating it. Laws immunizing religious corporations from discrimination charges may be experienced by orthodox believers as robust protection of their conscience; by others they may be experienced as a licence to discriminate, as treating LGBTs as second-class citizens. The 'mere knowledge' that the state has 'authorized' religious companies to discriminate against LGBTs may very well in itself be

---

70 Robert Wintemute, 'Accommodating Religious Beliefs: Harm Clothing or Symbols, and Refusals to Serve Others', 77:2 *Modern Law Review* (2014), pp. 223-253, at p. 241.

71 E. Anderson and R. Pildes, 'Expressive Theories of Law: A General Restatement', 148:5 *University of Pennsylvania Law Review* (2000), pp. 1503-1576, at p. 1527.

72 E.g. NeJaime and Siegel, *supra* note 1; Rosenfeld, *supra* note 61, at p. 92.

73 Expressive harm can also be caused more horizontally (private person versus private person) and by society at large, e.g. through bigoted acts, hatred and bullying (see also under B.4), but the focus here is on harm caused by public authorities.

felt as 'an affront to the dignity and worth of [LGBTs]'.[74] In this context, direct harm and especially expressive harm tend to be trivialized, ignored, or criticized for being difficult to measure.[75] Yet emerging socio-legal studies corroborate the theoretical concern of expressive harm with empirical proof. One such study investigating numerous laws at the municipal level providing religious exemptions from equal treatment requirements indicates that the direct discrimination in the areas concerned is significant and drastically fostered by such legislation.[76] This is hardly surprising since this is the very object of these laws: to license differential treatment, to 'allow people to elevate their prejudices above fairness and equality'.[77] Contrary to what advocates of religious exemption laws have claimed,[78] instances where these laws are put into use are not uncommon; rather in some places these laws find a ready demand not only in the service sector related to weddings, but also by 'child welfare agencies, physical and mental health providers and businesses that serve the public'.[79] Such laws 'enable and embolden businesses

---

74 Wintemute, *supra* note 70, p. 242, referencing *Marriage Commissioners Reference* 2011 SKCA 3 at 107.

75 E.g. Koppelman, *supra* note 58, p. 134-135 ('there is every reason to think that religious exemptions will not often be sought') and 136 ('[it is claimed] that gay people are hurt by every instance of discrimination ... But this is not precisely an argument. It is an assertion'); and Christopher McCrudden, 'Marriage Registrars, Same-Sex Relationships, and Religious Discrimination in the European Court of Human Rights', in Susanna Mancini and Michel Rosenfeld (eds.), *The Conscience Wars: Rethinking the Balance between Religion, Identity and Equality* (Cambridge: CUP, 2018), systematically ignoring or downplaying dignitary harms to LGBTs (see also concerns expressed about this by Robert Post at p. 482 in the same volume).

76 Human Rights Watch, *'All We Want is Equality' Religious Exemptions and Discrimination against LGBT People in the United States* (2018), based on interviews with 100 respondents in US states where religious exemption laws are in force.

77 *Ibid.*, p. 2.

78 E.g. Koppelman, *supra* note 58.

79 Human Rights Watch, *supra* note 68, p. 2.

and service providers to refuse to serve LGBT people, compelling LGBT people to invest additional time, money, and energy to find willing providers; others simply give up on obtaining the goods or services they need.[80] In addition to such instances of harm suffered through acts of direct discrimination, the phenomenon of expressive harm is thoroughly substantiated in the same study:

'More insidiously, they give LGBT people reason to expect discrimination before it even occurs, and to take extra precautions or avoid scenarios where they might face hostility out of self-preservation. Such laws also threaten the basic dignity of LGBT people, sending a clear message that their rights and well-being are not valued and are contingent on the goodwill of others ... [I]nterviewees explained that, by enacting religious exemptions to blunt the advancement of LGBT equality, lawmakers sent a powerful signal that they were unequal or unvalued in their community.'[81]

These data provide profound arguments against a priori legislative resolution of this human rights conflict in the form of blanket laws protecting conscience claims at all costs.

B4. *Context: Relative Vulnerability.* Perhaps the question of relative vulnerability should be perceived as aggravating factor in conjunction with expressive harm rather than an independent prioritization factor. That is, the negative ramifications of a law or judicial decision permitting private actors to deny their services to members of the public for religious reasons are exacerbated if the latter face discrimination, intolerance, hate crimes, or other forms of historical exclusion.[82] Conversely, the target

---

80 *Ibid.*, p. 3.
81 *Ibid.*, p. 3.
82 Rosenfelt, *supra* note 61, p. 92.

group could in theory also be very well established, tolerated and protected, with the conscientious objector belonging to a religious fringe group suffering forms of public and social discrimination, hostility and suspicion. This does not make the act of rejection on the part of the conscientious objector any less discriminatory, but it would be an indicator that the risk of expressive harm vis-à-vis the targeted group is relatively minor. Such sociological context analysis hardly ever features in case law. To wit, the European Court of Human Rights relied heavily on the margin of appreciation when assessing a labour conflict between a secular company and an individual religious employee who refused to provide the company's sexual counselling services to a lesbian couple; in this case, the employee was fired for refusing to provide the service. In the Court's opinion, what mattered a bit was that an equal treatment policy was in place when McFarlane, the employee, voluntarily joined the company (i.e. the *foreseeability* argument); and what mattered a lot was that the company's 'action was intended to secure the implementation of its policy of providing a service without discrimination'.[83] While the first argument stands to reason, the second fails to convince as such. The fact that an action aims to promote human rights in and of itself does not justify sacrificing another right. The only thing this proves is that a genuine restriction ground, namely 'the rights of others', was quite literally engaged through the company's equal opportunities policy. It does not prove *necessity* nor any careful weighing of all rights concerned. The question that seems to most forcefully present itself (yet is ignored by the Court) is: who, under the circumstances, stood to lose more, who was most vulnerable: Mr McFarlane or the same-sex couple rejected by him? Put differently, which party

---

83 *Eweida and others*, para. 109.

experiences the biggest setback in emancipation and tolerance? The religious practitioner who experiences repercussions if religiously motivated homophobia is brought to the workplace, or a homosexual who seeks private services but who is turned away, a refusal that (under a reverse outcome) would be tolerated by the company and accommodated by state authorities? It is contended the answer to this question differs from context to context, changes over time, and from place to place – forcing at all times a contemporaneous context-based assessment, and precluding at all times a priori settlements of such conflicts through blanket laws.

B5. *Public/private divide:* On the service side of our discussion, conscientious objections cannot be accommodated when they are expressed by actors that exercise public power. The public nature of the office that civil servants represent stands in the way of that. Any alternative argument renders LGBTs, upon whom taxes are also levied to fund these very same public offices, as second-class citizens. Even if a sensitive intake system might ultimately solve any access issues and even avoid direct in-your-face denials, the expressive harm flowing from the fact that state officers have an official licence to refuse services to part of the public as long as a stand-in is arranged would be overwhelming. Turning to the private sector, given that its services are commercial, full public funding would normally not be at stake here. That said, in numerous countries the private sector, whether for profit or not for profit, is involved in the delivery of some public goods, like education, healthcare, and so on, and occasionally these private entities get partial state funding. While such entities may have a conscience-driven wish to protect their religious autonomy and exert their ethos by stipulating service access conditions, the involvement of public money and public goods

stands in the way of that. A case in point were the British religious (mostly Catholic) adoption agencies, which were forced to
close down or sever their ties with the church as a result of laws
that stepped up the fight against discrimination of homosexuals
and their access to goods and services.[84]

---

84 2007 Sexual Orientation Regulations.

6. CONCLUDING REMARKS

I have argued that corporate freedom of religion can be legally supported with respect to sole proprietor companies and such *closely-held* companies as to make it genuinely possible to distil the conscience from the shareholder-owners. True, this concept as a legal notion may collide with other legal standards, notably the fundamental rights of others. It has been argued, however, that judges and lawyers ought to engage with those concerns about the rights of others whilst genuinely engaging with the merits of the collective religious freedom complaint. Not only does this do justice to all rights at stake, it makes for better judgements, gives to each its own, also to the losing camp, who are interested, in addition to an outright 'win', in being taken seriously and treated in accordance with principles of procedural fairness.[85] Ideally, in the long run this might prevent excessive juridification of the emerging 'conscience wars'.

I have argued that, for religious accommodations to be justifiable, companies must be closely held – they must moreover be transparent about their religious conscience. While equal treatment norms and the excessiveness of direct in your-face-discrimination will typically stand in the way of differential treatment of customers, internal HR-related ramifications of the corporate religious conscience vis-à-vis employees and prospective employees must be foreseeable in order to be permissible. Only then can the company's religious mission justifiably affect employment with this company. The most transparent approach

---

85　Brems, *supra* note 40, p. 281.

would be if employees were to know about this mission from the outset, i.e. upon or even prior to recruitment, through transparent recruiting and communication. Presumably, then, the workforce will closely mirror the closely-held company: both stakeholder base and workforce are relatively small, e.g. family or otherwise small businesses revolving around a business model of religiously likeminded persons. (Though in theory such a company could grow into a large one too if enough likeminded persons are willing to subscribe to the formula.) Obviously, as both law and religion are not immutable, not all conflicts can be anticipated. It would be harsh on religious autonomy to conclude that in all non-anticipated conflicts fair procedure automatically triumphs. Conversely, it would be equally harsh to conclude that the company has a carte blanche to rid itself of any individual employee the moment a religious loyalty conflict arises. The proportionality principle mitigates here, forcing the company to facilitate less interfering alternatives, for instance, by offering alternative positions in which the alleged 'disloyalty' is less disruptive to the religious mission of the company.

Mine, then, is above anything else a call for context-dependent, case-by-case resolution of pluralist rights conflicts and a firm stance against sweeping, a priori and blanket legislative settlements of rights collisions.[86] Those legislative 'solutions' to pluralist rights conflicts that immunize religious freedom from any encroachment that may occur within the pluralist state in particular ought to be firmly rejected. This holier-than-thou

---

86　See also UN Special Rapporteur on Freedom of Religion or Belief, A/HRC/7/10/ Add.3, para. 72 (and 47).

approach to religious freedom, emerging within domestic legislating arenas, should be rejected since there is no hierarchy of rights, and religious freedom, like many other fundamental rights, is not absolute.

Previously I have drawn on socio-legal research, with a selective focus,[87] charting the ramifications of sweeping 'licence to discriminate' laws. Human rights scholarship is in dire need of far more comprehensive socio-legal studies of this kind, covering all states that have introduced universal marriage freedom. Since the Netherlands first introduced the freedom to marry in 2001, over 25 liberal democracies have followed suit. All of these jurisdictions have been subject to intense political and academic debates on how to square that freedom with the conscience rights of others. While the different legal and judicial solutions are subject to scholarship, thus far we do not know much about the effects of such solutions on the everyday lives of both LGBTs and religionists.

I have proposed a dozen or so prioritization principles that help establish the 'necessity' of letting one right triumph over others. Positing that the present issue requires case-by-case, context-based assessment presupposes that my guidelines are not exhaustive. I have laid down the groundwork. Future cases are unpredictable and factual parallels and differences with this groundwork must be scrutinized for legal relevance, thus gradually filling in the patchwork of equitable human rights solutions to pluralist dilemmas.

---

87 The studies mentioned focus on the US.

My 'groundwork' also ostensibly omits certain factors. I find them to be irrelevant, particularly the *availability* argument.[88] The question of available alternatives has no validity within the service sector. The general availability of the service sought by for instance an LGBT does not impact the balancing of colliding rights. Given the nature of the direct harm suffered by the rejectee – the insulting nature of being rejected outright because of who you are – the fact that the next shop might not close its door on you, or the fact that the service at stake can be secured by driving a little further to the next town, does not prejudice that hardship has been incurred. Moreover, the notion of expressive harm has value in this context too. Should the existence of available alternatives legally/judicially matter as mitigating circumstances, as factors detracting from the discriminatory act and from the ostensible hardship experiences, the message to LGBTs essentially is: you should not complain so much, you have access to all public and private services, but you may need to walk a little further to secure that access. A second-class-citizen approach if ever there was one. Under such a model of sexual orientation apartheid, it is but small leap to arguing that LGBTs must manage their own hardship: they do not need to experience rejection, if they just make an effort to figure out where they will be welcomed with open arms or where doors are likely to be closed in their faces. Less rejection, then, is perhaps the net result, but so is a system that perpetuates social discrimination.

Finally, my groundwork does not include the factor of *sincerity*, however tempting this notion is. True enough, whether conveniently or coincidentally, the fact is that emerging corporate conscientious objections often pertain to generally applicable

---

88   E.g. proposed by McCrudden, *supra* note 67, pp. 457-458.

laws that cost the company revenue. Given the price of certain religious accommodations, it would be tempting to reject at least those conscientious claims that appear to be insincere. One major obstacle here, though, strikes at the core of religious autonomy and religious freedom, namely the fact that secular authorities are ill-positioned to delve into the precise significance or scope of concrete religious dictates and tenets, or to judge whether someone truly adheres to a certain belief or not. The same risk of insincerity first emerged in the context of individual conscientious objections to military service and other generally applicable laws where most jurisdictions have erred on the side of caution by introducing only very marginal assessments, if any, to ascertain whether the claimed religion is indeed held and whether the claimed religion is indeed fundamentally irreconcilable with the duty under applicable laws. The same principled choice in favour of generous religious freedom protection would seem to extend to the corporate equivalent of this freedom. Naturally, this does not prejudice the possibility of – fierce – scholarly, journalistic and other criticism in the face of conscience claims that appear, if not insincere, then at least opportunistic. For example, Hobby Lobby made vast investments – and makes a profit out of these investments – in the industries that produce the very same contraceptives it has objected to as part of its exemption claim vis-à-vis the contraceptive mandate.[89] In other words, it appears that Hobby Lobby objects to contraceptives only when it costs the company money. True, individuals are, for the purposes of recognizing conscience claims, not expected to be completely consistent or coherent

89 E.g. Molly Redden, 'Hobby Lobby's Hypocrisy: The Company's Retirement Plan Invests in Contraception Manufacturers', *Mother Jones* (1 April 2014); Heather Long, 'Hobby Lobby Does Invest in Birth Control', *CNN Money* (2 July 2014).

in the beliefs they hold either,[90] but Hobby Lobby's conscience seems to be particularly self-serving. Given that Hobby Lobby's most express if not exclusive religious practice to date has been its objection to the contraceptive mandate, and if the underlying objection is so dear to the company as it claims to be, it should be relatively straightforward for Hobby Lobby to streamline its corporate piety in this regard.

While short of Pandora's box, I do expect corporate religious conscience claims to further proliferate, thus appealing to *jurisprudence* to channel this development in a sensitive way, avoiding knee-jerk or otherwise sweeping legislative reactions. I have touched upon some of the dilemmas society, politics, and science will be faced with, emphasizing throughout mostly LGBT and women's rights. Not wholly unimaginable too will be inter-religious conscientious objections to mutual business relations, that is, one religious ethos-driven company not wishing to engage in contractual relationships with another company over the 'unacceptable' (from a religious viewpoint) policies in place within that company. Yet further proliferation is bound to occur, in fact is occurring, in this area when we take into account corporate 'counter-measures' – borrowing from international law's nomenclature – to corporate conscientious objections. In a sense these are *conscientious objections to conscientious objections*. These include secular objections too. An excellent example is provided by those domestic law societies that have decided, collectively, never to recruit lawyers from private universities that bar LGBTs. That policy decision is not only a reprisal, it is partly a substantive decision, the rationale being that those alumni are held to be more likely to have homophobic

---

90 Sepinwall, p. 183.

attitudes than alumni from more inclusive universities. This in turn sets off yet further relevant research of a socio-legal kind: what, indeed, are the social effects of any such corporate conscientious objections and what is the impact of public law, policy and case law in this area?

These are great times to be a law and religion scholar.